PROTECTING
OUR CHILDREN
TOGETHER

Minimizing the Psychological Harms of Racism

MELISSA LITTLE

© 2021 Melissa Little

All rights reserved. No part of this publication may be reproduced, distributed, or transmitted in any form or by any means, including photocopying, recording, or other electronic or mechanical methods, without the prior written permission of the publisher, except in the case of brief quotations embodied in critical reviews and certain other noncommercial uses permitted by copyright law.

ISBN Paperback: 978-0-578-85388-8

Cover and interior design: Andy Meaden meadencreative.com

This book is dedicated to my nephews, Nicholas and Jayden, and unborn children. May God put a hedge of protection around you. I love you with all my heart.

© 2021 Melissa Little

All rights reserved. No part of this publication may be reproduced, distributed, or transmitted in any form or by any means, including photocopying, recording, or other electronic or mechanical methods, without the prior written permission of the publisher, except in the case of brief quotations embodied in critical reviews and certain other noncommercial uses permitted by copyright law.

ISBN Paperback: 978-0-578-85388-8

Cover and interior design: Andy Meaden meadencreative.com

MELISSA A. LITTLE
CONSULTING &
MEDIATION SERVICES

CHANGING MINDS | RESTRUCTURING SYSTEMS | EMPOWERING COMMUNITIES | RESOLVING CONFLICTS

CONTENTS

INTRODUCTION

"If you have to get on your knees and bow when a White person goes past, do it willingly." —Mamie Till

In 1955, Emmet Till, a fourteen-year-old boy, was leaving his home in Chicago to visit family in Mississippi when his mother gave him "the talk." For the safety of her son, Ms. Mamie Till explained to Emmet how to act in the South while in the presence of Whites. Embedded in her warning was that White people were to be treated differently—with a higher level of respect—superior. In an effort to survive, Black families were forced to have these degrading talks with their children in hopes that their actions would not result in them being jailed or lynched. Despite these tough conversations, being taught how to function in the segregated South was not a guarantee that one would survive. On August 24, 1955, Emmet was brutally murdered and disfigured for allegedly flirting with a White woman—an allegation that was later found to be untrue. An all-White jury acquitted the murderers.

Now, sixty-five years later, Black parents, and those who help raise Black children (collectively, "parental figures"), still bear the heavy burden of teaching their loved ones the "proper" way to act, dress, and talk to Whites—particularly law enforcement—in hopes that these acts will mollify their dark skin, which can be seen as threatening. In 2014, David Miller, created an infographic "10 Rules of Survival if Stopped by the Police," a modern-day approach to keep Black children and youth alive during police encounters.

1. Be polite and respectful when stopped by the police. Keep your mouth closed.

2. Remember that your goal is to get home safely. If you feel that your rights have been violated, you and your parents have the right to file a formal complaint with your local police jurisdiction.

3. Don't, under any circumstance, get into an argument with the police.

4. Always remember that anything you say or do can be used against you in court.

5. Keep your hands in plain sight and make sure the police can see your hands at all times.

6. Avoid physical contact with the police. No sudden movements and keep hands out of your pockets.

7. Do not run, even if you are afraid of the police.

8. Even if you believe that you are innocent, do not resist arrest.

9. Don't make any statements about the incident until you are able to meet with a lawyer or public defender.

10. Stay calm and remain in control. Watch your words, body language and emotions.

These rules, or some variation, are taught in many civic organizations that work with black and brown youth—including in my own church. Sadly, being respectful and keeping one's hands in the air are not always enough to protect Black children from unlawful arrests or from being murdered. Nevertheless, these lessons help improve the likelihood that they will return home alive—and therefore are necessary. On the other hand, these survival lessons can lead to Black children developing an inferiority complex.

The purpose of this book is to provide guidance on how parental figures can have "the talk" with their children, while minimizing the psychological harm. This book encourages parental figures to have conversations with their children about race starting at a young age; explains how to do so in a manner that educates, empowers, and instills pride; and provides advice on what parental figures can do before and after racist events.

1

WHY TALKING WITH YOUNG CHILDREN ABOUT RACE IS NECESSARY

Racial Awareness Begins at an Early Age

Several years ago, my cousin, a dark-skinned woman, was walking down a grocery store aisle when a little White girl noticed her and yelled out, "Mommy look, she is Black." The mother replied, "Yes — isn't she beautiful." With only four words, the mother normalized the difference between her skin tone and the skin tone of my cousin. In that moment, the young girl learned that people who do not look like her are beautiful people too.

Young children are often curious when they encounter a racially diverse person, if they are not use to seeing people from that racial group. They have questions and are looking to the adults in their lives to help fill in the blanks. Unfortunately, many parental figures often miss these opportunities to enlighten children about the beauty of diversity, due to fear of saying the wrong thing and/or being viewed as a racist. For other parental figures, there is the belief that speaking with young children about race at an early age is counterintuitive, unnecessary, or even harmful, when the goal is to shelter and protect the innocence of children for as long as possible. These positions of avoidance are based on at least three inherently flawed assumptions:

1. Teaching your children not to verbally acknowledge racial differences makes you and your children less racist.

2. It is best not to say anything when you do not have all the answers.

3. Children will not develop racial awareness or social attitudes about race until you, the parental figure, are ready to have that conversation or until children get older and learn about race and racial social constructs for themselves.

To the contrary, as Dunham, Baron, and Banaji remark, as early as infancy, babies prefer the face and voice of their primary caregiver, familiar dialect, and faces of racial ingroup members. As the authors continue, "White six-year-olds in the US manifested implicit ingroup preference at levels statistically identical to White American adults."[1]

There have been many studies over the years that show young children not only recognize racial differences at infancy but begin forming attitudes about race based upon their social learning environments. Because of the stark racial disparities in housing, education, health care, and the criminal justice system, as well as personal discrimination, what many children hear and observe in their natural environments often lead to Black children feeling inferior and White children feeling superior. Dating back to the 1940s, the infamous Clark doll study revealed the psychological harm of living in a racially segregated and unequal society. In that study, Black children as young as three years old were able to identify the race of the dolls, their own race, the dolls they perceived to be nice, the bad dolls, and the dolls they preferred. Most of these children rejected the black or brown doll and described positive characteristics to the white doll.

Similar research, conducted by William, Boswell and Best in 1975, showed that approximately three-quarters of White children in preschool through second grade had a very favorable view of White Americans and a negative view of African Americans. Black children in first grade also showed a pro-White bias and a negative Black bias, although to a lesser degree. At each grade level studied, there was a significantly higher pro-White and negative Black mindset than there was a pro-Black and negative White one. In the same report, Hispanic children as young as five years old growing up in a predominantly Hispanic neighborhood showed no preference for their ingroup when compared with White children. However, these same children did show ingroup preference when comparing their group to Black Americans.[2]

Sadly, not much has changed since then. In 2005, as reflected in an eight-minute documentary, *A Girl Like Me*, Black children, when asked, were still contributing negative traits with Black dolls and themselves.

"Can you show me the doll that looks bad?"

The young Black girl selects the Black doll over the White doll.

"And why does that look bad?"

"Because she's Black,"

"And why is this the nice doll?"

"Because she's White."

"And can you give me the doll that looks like you?"

The little girl pushes forward the Black doll.[3]

In 2010, a pilot study from CNN, looked at White and Black children of different age groups and showed that White children responded by identifying the color of their own skin with positive attributes and darker skin with negative attributes. Black children also had some bias toward White skin, but far less than White children.[4]

Negative Biases Can Be Learned and Reinforced in Schools

The Clark doll study from the 1940s is still relevant because racism is still intertwined in the fabric of America and all its systems. This includes our education system. In a more recent study, comprised of 5,147 fifth-grade students and their parents, 15 percent of children reported perceived racial/ethnic discrimination, with 80 percent reporting that discrimination occurred at school.[5]

Since the day my nephew was born, my sister, a clinical psychologist, spent countless hours trying to figure out ways to shield her son from the racial biases and prejudices that many Black children experience in school. She understood, like many parental figures do, that these bad experiences can lead to serious, immediate, and long-term consequences. Data supports these concerns:

- In 2017, racial harassment complaints in schools increased by nearly 25 percent nationwide.[6]

- Across California, during the 2017-18 school year, 14 percent of public high school students said they had experienced bullying or harassment due to their race, ethnicity, or national origin in the past twelve months.[7]

Researcher Caryn C. Park conducted a study inside of the classroom using students three-and-a-half to five-and-a-half years old.[8] Roughly a quarter of the students were children of color, yet they accounted for half of the classroom exclusions that were observed by the researcher. This included an African American/Latina girl named Kayla, who tried to initiate play with two white girls. The White girls shouted at her to go away. Kayla moved closer to those girls and one of them kicked an object that caused Kayla to fall. Kayla got up and walked away without notifying the teacher. Other examples of exclusion included refusing to look or touch an object that was brought in by a student of color during "show-and-tell" or selecting the student of color as the villain in make-believe play.

The data further shows that Black children are treated differently in the school system by adults and are often held to a different standard, even if it is unintentional. Researchers at the Yale University Child Study Center asked more than 130 preschool teachers to watch video clips of children in classrooms.[9] These teachers were told to look for signs of "challenging behavior." The children in the videos were actors, and the clips did not actually show any challenging behaviors. Based upon the equipment that tracked their gaze, the findings revealed that preschool teachers spent more time looking at Black children than White children, especially Black boys. Another study conducted in 2014 showed Black boys, by the age of ten, are more likely to be viewed as older and more culpable/less innocent than White peers.[10] A report by Georgetown Law's Center on Poverty and Inequality, "Girlhood Interrupted: The Erasure of Black Girls' Childhood," revealed similar results for young Black girls.[11] Beginning at age five, adults in the United States view Black girls as less innocent and older than White girls. Compared to White girls of the same age, the participants perceived that Black girls need less nurturing, less protection, less support, and less comfort and that they are more independent, know more about adult topics, and know more about sex.

This is particularly concerning when it comes to school discipline:

- Disparities in school suspension rates between White students and students of color occur even in preschool-aged children.[12]

- Although studies fail to show that Black students misbehave at higher rates than White students, Black students are three times more likely to be suspended or expelled.[13]

- A 2002 study found that White students were more likely to be disciplined for nondiscretionary offenses such as smoking, vandalism, and obscene language, while Black students were more likely to be disciplined for discretionary acts such as disrespect.[14]

- These disciplinary referrals can often lead to more serious or traumatic events, such as long-term suspension or referrals to law enforcement.

- In 2011-12, Black children made up 16 percent of all children enrolled in schools; however, they accounted for 31 percent of all in-school arrests.[15]

In addition to being treated differently, excluded, bullied, and harassed, many Black children are denied educational opportunities and are taught from a Eurocentric framework that minimizes the contributions, culture, and achievements of people of African descent. According to the National Center for Education Statistics, there are nearly double the percentage of White students compared to Black students who are in the talented and gifted program.[16] Data in 2009 from the U.S. Department of Education Office for Civil Rights reveal that African American students constituted 16.7 percent of the student population, but just 9.8 percent of students in gifted programs.[17] Similarly, Hispanic students made up 22.3 percent of students but only 15.4 percent of students receiving gifted services.[18] By contrast, Black students are twice as likely than White students to be labeled as emotionally and intellectually disabled.[19]

Parental Figures Have the Power to Build and Restore Good Self-Esteem and a Healthy Identity

The data is clear: children are not color blind, nor do they live in a color-blind society. In contrast, children learn at an early age that certain groups of people are more valued in society than others. Consequently, failing to discuss race with your children and help them understand the beauty of who they are can be detrimental to their psychological well-being. Parental figures have the advantage to instill self-pride in young children, prior to any event that calls into question their true value and worth. As parental figures, your power is not withdrawing from the harsh realities of racism; your power is in teaching your children the truth about their Africanness before the world tries to define it for them.

2
HOW TO HAVE APPROPRIATE CONVERSATIONS WITH CHILDREN ABOUT RACISM

Connecting with Children at Their Level to Discuss Racism

When speaking children about racism, it is important to be honest and to tailor the discussion to the age of the child. For younger children, these conversations should start with lessons on valuing diversity and differences and treating all people with fairness. This can be accomplished by using simple language, such as "We all are beautiful," "We all are God's children," "Everyone is special and unique." Within those conversations, you can explain that not everyone shares these same values and as a result may treat people poorly due to the color of their skin. Your children should understand that these acts of intolerance are not okay and that they should tell you, and other trusted adults, if they are made to feel that way. To better understand what your children may be experiencing or feeling it is always helpful to ask them open-ended questions:

"Tell me more about that"

"Why do you think that happened"

"What would you have done differently"

"How did that make you feel"

"How do you think that made others feel".

When it comes to discussions with young children about police and the mistreatment of Black people, the same method or strategies can be applied. Start by explaining the role of good police officers and the benefits of good community policing. Similarly, use simple and direct language to discuss racism and police misconduct. If there is a particular police incident that happened in your community, or an event that you would like to talk with your children about, you can start by asking them open-ended questions. Allow your children's responses to guide your conversations. This should be an open dialogue that is tailored to meet your children where they are at. At the end of these conversations, reassure your children that they are loved and that you, and a community of friends and family, are there to keep them safe.

As your children get older, continue to create an environment where they feel secure and comfortable sharing their thoughts about race topics with you. Because many older adolescents are exposed to social media and are aware of racial incidents that have been highly publicized, have open dialogues with your children about those events. Race talks with older adolescents should be more involved and include topics such as individual racism, institutional racism, and implicit bias. Older adolescents should understand that racism and implicit bias might cause police officers to view them as older and more threatening than their white peers. To enhance your discussions on racial injustice, consider sharing research, reading pertinent books together, and watching movies/documentaries. These additional resources can also be used to highlight the resiliency, strength, and power of African people.[20]

Discussing Historical Facts to Build Self-Pride, Courage, and Hope

Embedded in your race discussions should be lessons about the rich history and beauty of African/African American culture. There is power when children know where they come from, and that they were created for a purpose. Part of that history includes precolonial African kingdoms, the strength and accomplishments of African people while enslaved, documented slave revolts, the reconstruction period (1863-77), the rise and fall of Black banks and Black townships (Black Wall Street), the civil rights movement, and the many achievements of modern-day Black men and women. Sadly, many adults lack a true understanding and knowledge of African/African American history and culture for various reasons. As a result, many parental figures must first learn about African history to accurately teach their children. If you do not have the time to read multiple books about Black history and culture, consider listening to podcasts while engaging in other activities that allow you to multi-task, such as driving, cleaning, or working out. You can also watch YouTube videos or documentaries on these topics. There are many ways to learn more about the history of African people that is conducive to your lifestyle. The story of the African people is one of victory, strength, triumph, grace, love, and determination, and our children must be taught that these qualities and traits are also embedded in their DNA.

Furthermore, when discussing racism with young people, it is important that they understand they are not powerless—and that there are historical figures who they can look to for guidance and inspiration when they are searching for solutions to address a wrong. The civil rights movement is an example of what young people can do with limited resources, using intellectual strategy, peaceful demonstrations, and active organizing. Individuals and student groups such as the Student Nonviolent Coordinating Committee, the Little Rock 9; the Greensboro 4, Ruby Bridges, the Birmingham Children's Crusades, and so many others were instrumental in changing America for the better. There are also modern-day activists, grassroot organizers, and leaders from all over the world in different professions who are challenging injustices and using their talents, gifts, and platforms to make the world a little better. Tell your children about how these ordinary people are doing extraordinary things to bring about change and equality.

Identifying Personal Talents Will Help to Empower Children When Faced with Adversities

In addition to sharing stories about how other activists are making a difference, it is just as important that your children understand that they too have gifts and talents to make this world a better place. This starts with sincere verbal affirmations every day to your children that they are special, loved, beautiful, intelligent, and purposefully made and that you are proud of who they are.

In school and at home, adults have a tendency to hyper-focus on children's weaknesses, resulting in children who feel more comfortable identifying their shortcomings than their strengths. This leads to feelings of inadequacy and low self-esteem. Although we should work with our children to help improve in these areas, just as much time, if not more, time should be spent developing their gifts and helping them to see the value in those gifts. When this occurs, the impact of negative influences are greatly reduced.

Daily affirmations that they are strong, smart, resilient, and beautiful help rebut the negative messaging that they are continuously receiving. Yet, more is required than just positive declarations from parental figures. Children must see for themselves that they are special through personal experiences. This is no different for adults who feel more accomplished, smarter, and more resilient when they complete a hard task or goal or overcome an obstacle. These experiences help adults push through other challenges and set new goals with higher expectations. The same is true for young people. Your children should not only know that you believe they are beautifully and wonderfully made, but they too must be able to identify their own talents and gifts, as well as understand why their talents are valuable. One way for your child to learn more about themselves is by giving them age-appropriate responsibilities. This will allow them to see that there are some things that they can do independently and that their actions can positively impact others. Volunteering in the community— at a local church, food bank, nursing home, or a charity of choice—will further boost self-confidence. Children, like adults, feel good about themselves and are empowered when they do good for their families and communities.

Older youth can learn more about what they can do to improve their communities through internships and sitting on a government board or commission as a student representative. It is important for youth to understand the political process, how their government body works, who has the power to make laws and policies, the important role of informed voters/active citizenship, the power of their activism, and how their voice matters. Encourage your children to write letters to their local officials regarding matters that are important to them. These experiences will help to build self-confidence, leadership qualities, and a belief that they too have the ability to change things for the better. This type of foundation will be beneficial in those moments when your child may otherwise feel helpless after a racist incident.

Preparing Children for Police Encounters

When it is time to have discussions with your children about police encounters, your children should first know and understand that they too have rights under the law. When and how they exercise those rights, however, will depend on the situation. According to organizations such as Black Youth Project[21] and the American Civil Liberties Union (ACLU), you should consider the following if stopped for questioning by the police:

1. You can assert your right to remain silent by saying so out loud. This means once you have clearly asserted this right you do not have to answer the police officer's questions. However, in some states you may still be required to provide your name, address, and date of birth.

2. You do not have to consent to a search of yourself or your belongings. However, if suspected of carrying a concealed weapon, police may "pat-down" your clothing. Although you cannot physically resist, you should calmly state that you do not consent to any search.

3. If you are under arrest, you have a right to know why and should ask. If arrested, you have a right to a lawyer.

4. Do not become verbally or physically aggressive or run away, even if you frightened or believe what is happening is unreasonable. This could lead to more serious consequences.

To help your children better understand what they should do during police encounters, go over with your children the ten rules of survival discussed earlier in this book.

1. Be polite and respectful when stopped by the police. Keep your mouth closed.

2. Remember that your goal is to get home safely. If you feel that your rights have been violated, you and your parents have the right to file a formal complaint with your local police jurisdiction.

3. Do not, under any circumstance, get into an argument with the police.

4. Always remember that anything you say or do can be used against you in court.

5. Keep your hands in plain sight and make sure the police can see your hands at all times.

6. Avoid physical contact with the police. No sudden movements and keep hands out of your pockets.

7. Do not run, even if you are afraid of the police.

8. Even if you believe that you are innocent, do not resist arrest.

9. Don't make any statements about the incident until you are able to meet with a lawyer or public defender.

10. Stay calm and remain in control. Watch your words, body language, and emotions.

Role-playing can also be beneficial. For example, have your children practice saying that they wish to remain silent and would like to speak with an attorney before answering any additional questions. Unfortunately, because some officers may disregard your children's constitutional rights and act improperly, train your children to remain calm and tell them that a formal complaint can be filed once they are safely home. If your children are arrested, they should again be instructed to assert their right to speak with an attorney. As part of your role-play, also include action steps that can be taken to address the police officer's improper conduct. This framework prepares Black children for racist encounters with the police without stripping them of their humanity by forcing them to simply accept the status quo.

Due to the presence of police officers in many schools across America, it is just as important to speak with your children about how to interact with police officers/school resource officers in the school setting. Young people's rights will be different in the school setting than in a non-school setting. For example, a *school official* does not need probable cause or a warrant to search a student. Nevertheless, your children still have rights when interacting with school officials or school police. The school official must have "reasonable suspicion" to justify conducting the search unless the student provides consent. This may also be true for certain school resource officers. Your children should know what their rights are and the best way to advocate for themselves based upon the setting and environment. This includes your children's right to remain silent. It is important to remember that school misconduct can also result in criminal charges and that in-school statements can also be used against your children in criminal proceedings. Parental figures should be familiar with their children's school policies and handbooks, including those pertaining to school discipline and role of school police officers.

Responding to Your Child After the Racist Event

When your children are treated unfairly because of their race or they witness a racist incident, naturally they will experience a wide range of emotions. The hope is that the lessons that you have ingrained in them over the years will overcome whatever negative emotions they are feeling and that they will find positive ways to deal with their hurt, pain, shame, and/or anger. This is not the time to have your first conversation with them about racism. Rather, this is the time to be sympathetic and try to understand what your children may be feeling and what they are going through, before offering any advice. Listening and asking open-ended questions to try to understand what happened, validating their feelings, and simply being there can go a long way. Continue to check in with your children to ensure that they are okay and that steps are being taken to restore good mental health. For some children, part of the healing process includes a discussion on ways to address the racist conduct that occurred. For other children, waiting a few days to have a constructive conversation about possible solutions to address what has occurred may be necessary. In the meantime, the situation may require you, as the parental figure, to take immediate action. Your actions as a parental figure should not preclude you from also brainstorming with your children on how they would like to improve the situation.

Below are some suggestions to consider if your children encounter or witness a racist event. This list is intended to be a starting point and hopefully will trigger some additional ideas.

- Help your children find ways to best express their feelings.

- Find ways to restore your children's self-esteem.

- Ask your children to come up with ideas on how they can make the situation better or prevent similar incidents in the future.

- If the situation is serious, let your children know that the incident will need to be reported to proper officials (i.e., police or school administrators).

- Put your complaints in writing and meet with school staff.

- File a formal complaint with the school or a government agency, such as the Office of Civil Rights.

- Follow the complaint procedures at your school, including for title VI and VII violations.

- Get other parents and students involved in community activism.

- Consider mediation or other restorative justice practices.

- Reach out to school board members, the school superintendent, and other local officials.

- Find a therapist trained in, or who recognizes, race-based mental health problems.

- File a police complaint.

- Consult with an attorney.

3

UNDERSTANDING THE IMPACT OF RACISM ON YOUR CHILDREN'S MENTAL AND PHYSICAL HEALTH

Black Children Need More Support to Maintain Good Mental Health

People of African descent not only experience personal racial discrimination, but many also have to deal with systemic racism carried out through institutional policies. Although Black people's experiences with racism may vary, institutional racism and individual racism takes a toll on Black mental health, regardless of one's economic status or gender.

- In 2017, Blacks represented 12 percent of the U.S. adult population but 33 percent of the sentenced prison population.[22]

- Nationally, Black adults are roughly five times as likely to be incarcerated than White adults. In twelve states, more than half of the prison population is black: Alabama, Delaware, Georgia, Illinois, Louisiana, Maryland, Michigan, Mississippi, New Jersey, North Carolina, South Carolina, and Virginia. Maryland, whose prison population is 72 percent African American, tops the nation.[23]

- Blacks are shot and killed by the police at a rate that is over twice as high for White Americans.[24]

- Black children are six times as likely as White children to have had an imprisoned parent.[25]

- Black youth are more than five times as likely to be detained or committed compared to White youth.[26]

- In six states, African American youth are at least ten times as likely to be held in placement as are White youth: New Jersey, Wisconsin, Montana, Delaware, Connecticut, and Massachusetts.[27]

- While 14 percent of all youth under eighteen in the United States are Black, 42 percent of boys and 35 percent of girls in juvenile facilities are Black.[28]

These injustices are also found in America's health care, housing, and education systems. Nationwide, Black mother are three times more likely to die from complications in childbirth than White mothers. In New York City, the rate is twelve times as high for Black mothers than White mothers.[29] In housing, the gap between Black and White homeownership is greater now than in 1968, when housing discrimination was legal.[30] And in education, Black children are more than twice as likely as White children to attend high-poverty schools.[31]

These statistics are alarming—and can cause much anxiety for both Black children and their parental figures. These systemic injustices often result in experiences that are unhealthy, unsafe, and traumatic. Additionally, these traumas caused by racism can be passed down from generation to generation. According to recent epigenetic studies, racism and other traumas experienced in someone's lifetime can play a part in altering gene activity, and that change can be passed down from generation to generation. Common traumatic stress reactions due to racial trauma can include "increased vigilance and suspicion, increased sensitivity to threat, sense of a foreshortened future, and more maladaptive responses to stress such as aggression or substance use."[32] Exposure to racism can also lead to an increase in attention deficit hyperactivity disorder, anxiety, and depression, regardless of socioeconomic background.[33] In more serious cases, and if left untreated, anxiety, low self-esteem, and depression can lead to further health conditions; social, educational, or behavioral problems; or even suicide.

The statistics concerning suicide among Black youth are worth considering:

- From 1980-95, the suicide rate among African Americans ages 10 to 14 increased 233 percent, as compared to 120 percent of non-Hispanic Whites.

- Suicide attempts rose by 73 percent between 1991-2017 for Black adolescents (male and female), while injury by attempt rose by 122 percent for Black adolescent boys during that time period [34]

- Black youth are less likely to report suicidal thoughts but more likely to attempt suicide; Black males are more likely to suffer injury or death as a result.[35]

"Our story is one of perseverance and resilience. After all, we survived slavery; surely, we can survive 'sadness' or 'anxiety.' In this mindset, anything less would be considered spiritual or moral weakness."[36]

Despite these statistics, Black people are less likely than their White counterparts to receive the mental health supports that they need. In 2018, 58.2

percent of Black adults between the ages 18-25 and 50.1 percent of adults ages 26-49, with serious mental illness, did not receive treatment.[37] In part, this is due to the long-standing stigma concerning mental health illness in the Black community. This stigma is rooted in slavery, religion, and a mistrust of medical doctors. According to the National Alliance on Mental Health, many Black people rely solely on faith, family, and social communities for emotional support when mental health supports may also be necessary.[38] Many Black Christians believe that mental health supports are a sign of weakness or signifies a lack of faith. Additionally, many Black children and families do not receive the mental health supports that they require due to issues with treatment or lack of access to quality mental health providers. As a result, warning signs that require special attention are more likely to be ignored, or alternatively, children who require these extra supports are instead punished at home and in school.

In the school setting, research shows that the response to Black and Hispanic children exhibiting mental health symptoms, which can include behavioral problems, is often school punishment.

"Black middle and high school students are over three times more likely to attend a school with more security staff than mental health personnel, with 4.2 percent of white students and 13.1 percent of black students attending such schools."[39] Consequently, in addition to other societal pressures, Black children are forced to deal with insurmountable stressors related to racism without the proper mental health supports that are needed.

Proactive Measures to Reduce the Harmful Effects of Racism

Based on the data, parental figures must become more in-tune with the state of their children's mental health. As parental figures, you must help your children process what has occurred, why it occurred, and what they can do about it. To be able to go through this process, parental figures must first be aware that a racial encounter took place. Your children need to feel comfortable sharing with you confusing, painful, and even embarrassing events that they experience or witness. Simply because you are the parental figure does not necessarily mean that you are the "go to" trusted adult in your children's lives. These types of relationships are built based upon parental figures intentionally setting time aside to have open dialogue in a safe environment—way before the racial incident occurred. These conversations can be natural for you and your children to discuss, particularly when they begin at a young age.

If, however, your children are older, it is not too late to begin forming a relationship that encourages such intimate conversations. Try to meet your children where they are at—understand their comfort level and learning style. Sometimes as the parental figure, in order for your children to open up and be vulnerable about their real-life experiences, you also must be willing to let your guard down. It can be therapeutic for you and your child to hear about your personal childhood and adult experiences—for you to share your feelings, what you did to improve the situation or to improve yourself (how you may have "healed"), or, in some cases, what you still are trying to do to heal or improve the situation. These conversations should always be personalized based upon the age and maturity of the child. Additionally, surrounding your children with other positive adults and good friends and putting them in community programs (i.e., community sports and church) can mitigate the harmful effects of stress that come from adverse childhood experiences.[40]

Furthermore, teach your children ways that they can channel negative emotions into positive energy. For some children, this may be engaging in certain activities such as writing in a journal, drawing, running, or singing to help restore or maintain emotional stability. Regardless of your children's preferred activities, parental figures should encourage positive stress relievers every time their children feel upset until it becomes second nature. These behaviors should be encouraged and reinforced throughout the child's life. For children with emotional disabilities or those who struggle with self-regulation, get them the support that they need early. This may require professional guidance from a psychologist or a behavioral support professional. A school psychologist or school counselor/social worker could also be a resource when looking for supports and strategies that can be used in the home setting.

In sum, racism is tough on the mind and body. For many Black families in America, race-based stressors are constant, whether personally experienced or witnessed. Inevitably, the pressures and stressors that are placed on Black children have a direct impact on their mental health. According to Mental Health America, there are signs to look for when professional help may be needed. Some of these signs includes:

- Decline in school performance

- Poor grades despite strong efforts

- Constant worry or anxiety

- Repeated refusal to go to school or to take part in normal activities

- Hyperactivity or fidgeting

- Persistent nightmares

- Persistent disobedience or aggression

- Frequent temper tantrums

- Depression, sadness, or irritability[41]

If you are concerned about your child's mental health or believe they may benefit from counseling, seek out professional help from a trained therapist that recognizes race-based trauma. The Congressional Black Caucus identified in its 2019 report the following resources:[42]

- National Alliance on Mental Illness: nami.org
- National Organization for People of Color Against Suicide: nopcas.org
- The Society for the Prevention of Teen Suicide: sptsusa.org
- Suicide Prevention Resource Center: sprc.org
- The Trevor Project Lifeline: thetrevorproject.org
- Therapy for Black Men: therapyforblackmen.org
- Therapy for Black Girls: therapyforblackgirls.com

4

HOW TO BE A
GOOD GATEKEEPER

Minimizing the Impact of the Negative Messaging

One MLK weekend, my then five-year-old nephew was briefly exposed to a news program that showed Donald Trump calling African nations "shit holes." It did not occur to my sister that her son, who at the time was playing with his toys, had cued into the news program and heard the then leader of this country spewing out hateful rhetoric. But later that day, my nephew expressed that he did not want to visit the White House because "President Trump does not like Black people." He went further to ask when Barack Obama would become president again.

Most parental figures work hard and do their best to block their children from receiving negative messages that aim to dehumanize or devalue Black lives. Despite their best attempts, however, parental figures are not omnipresent. Inevitably, children of African descent will be exposed to hateful messaging that depict people of color as inferior, criminal, and/ or unintelligent. However, as you speak truth to your children about their Africanness, explain to your children that not everything they read and/or see in books, television, and social media is accurate, and that they must use their critical thinking skills to question those things that do not align with what they know to be true – that they are intelligent, beautiful, and wonderfully made.

Identifying and Filtering Out Negative Messaging

Negative messaging comes in many forms—word of mouth, television, video games, social media, books, and magazines. According to an article by Travis Nixon published in *Color of Change*, Blacks are more likely to be depicted as unstable and a burden to society.[43]

- News and opinion media overrepresent Black families receiving welfare by 18 percentage points.

- News media overrepresent the incidence of Black family poverty by 32 percentage points and underrepresent White family poverty by 49 percentage points.

- News and opinion media depict Black fathers as absent in the lives of their children, despite their being little evidence to suggest this. Even in cases in which Black fathers are living separately from their children, they are more likely to be involved in their children's lives than White fathers.[44]

- News media overrepresent Black family members as criminal by 11 percentage points. On the other hand, news media underrepresent White family members as criminal by 39 percentage points (28 percent of those represented as criminal are White family members, though White family members constitute 77 percent of those arrested for criminal activity, according to crime reports).

Likewise, when it comes to video games, Black characters are either seen as violent or athletic. In a study using over 149 games, 100 percent of Black males were portrayed as either athletic, violent, or both.[45]

Nevertheless, according to a Northwestern University report, minority youth aged eight to eighteen consume television/media at significantly higher rates than their White peers.[46]

- Black youth watch an average of nearly six hours of TV a day on various platforms (5:54), Hispanic youth close to five-and-a-half hours (5:21), Asian youth more than four-and-a-half hours (4:41), and White youth about three-and-a-half hours (3:36).

- Black and Hispanic youth are more likely to have a television in their bedrooms (84 percent of Blacks and 77 percent of Hispanics, compared to 64 percent of Whites and Asians) and to have cable and premium channels available in their bedrooms (42 percent of Blacks and 28 percent of Hispanics, compared to 17 percent of Whites and 14 percent of Asians).

- Minority youth eat more meals in front of the TV set (78 percent of Black, 67 percent of Hispanic, 58 percent of White, and 55 percent of Asian youth report that the TV is usually on during meals at home).

Furthermore, regardless of ethnicities and socioeconomic backgrounds, youth who spend more time on computers, tablets, and/or smartphones, and engage in high levels of social media use, have increased levels of depressive symptoms and suicide-related outcomes.[47]

As parental figures, you can curtail some of the negative images and information impacting your children's psychological and emotional well-being simply by limiting their consumption of television, social media, and video games, and installing parental control apps where appropriate. Overall, parental figures must be intentional about what they allow their children to watch, listen to, and read. Limiting your children's television and social media consumption will not only decrease the amount of negative messaging that they are exposed to but will hopefully encourage alternative healthy pastimes like getting exercise, reading, playing outside, writing in a journal, or engaging in science, technology, engineering, and math activities.

Connecting with Positive Community Members to Combat Negative Messaging

To support good emotional well-being, your children should also be around other people or part of organizations that reinforce the messaging that they are receiving inside of the home. You must be intentional about the organizations and after-school programs you put your children in. The people who you allow around your children should be people who will encourage and build up their self-esteem. If you are a part of an organization that serves children and youth, find ways to incorporate programs where children can learn and feel good about who they are and where they come from. Alternatively, look up different organizations or cultural events in your community to determine what would be a good fit for you and your children. If none of these options are available, consider starting your own.

- Participate in community events that are designed to build your children's self-esteem (i.e., youth groups, vacation Bible school, sports leagues, African dance troupe, "rites of passage" programs).

- Find ways to incorporate programs where children can learn about their history and feel good about who they are and where they come from.

- Organize a community event and utilize social media as your platform to connect with other families with similar interests.

Your Own Biases May Be Negatively Impacting Your Children

Parental figures must also be cognizant of how your actions may negatively impact your children. Consider the complicated concept of "code switching." According to National Public Radio, code switching is the practice of shifting the languages you use or the way you express yourself in your conversations.[48] For people of African descent, code switching is much more involved and can include adjusting one's appearance—such as hair or style of dress, behavior, and/or dialect in hopes of gaining acceptance by Whites, being treated fairly, securing a job, or even physical survival. Consequently, code switching is simply a part of life for many Black people. Not only is this psychologically damaging and exhausting for Black adults, but Black children observing these daily actions may conclude that their authentic self is not good enough. It is important for your children to know that Black beauty and Black intelligence is the norm, and their African essence is not something that they need to hide or downplay to fit in. Children growing up to believe that they are special because they are different than the "other

Black people" or better because they have been chosen by Whites as the acceptable Black person is unhealthy and creates a false sense of self-pride.

Moreover, as parental figures, you too are constantly being fed messaging intended to tear you down and to make you feel inferior. Consequently, you must also make a deliberate effort to understand your decisions, control your actions, educate yourself about your history, and continue to build yourself up.

5
LEAD BY EXAMPLE

Practice Self-Love and Showing Love to Others

You cannot expect for your children to see their beauty, and take pride in who they are, if you do not have a positive perspective about yourself.

It is not always enough to just tell a child that they are beautiful, smart, and just as good as their peers. In addition to providing history lessons and helping identify their talents and gifts, you must lead by your actions. As parental figures, if you want your children to respect others, learn to control their emotions, filter out negative energy, and love who they are, you must show them through your example. As parental figures, you are your children's first teachers and role models. How do you love yourself? How do you love your family? How do you love your neighbors? How do you treat people who are perceived as different? How do you let others treat you? How do you handle conflict? How do you show leadership? Answering these questions requires some self-reflection, which will hopefully lead to self-correction—working on being the person who you would want your children to see and emulate. As you begin to detoxify your mind, remember that not everyone is going through this process with you. As a result, it is important to monitor what others say and do around your children as well.

Find Positive Ways to Channel Negative Energy

As parental figures, it is important to recognize how the stresses of racism affect your life and how you choose to respond. Without question, dealing with all these societal ills and having to worry about your children's safety and well-being can be overwhelming at times. The thought of Tamar Rice, Travon Martin, Rayshard Brooks, Breonna Taylor, Eric Garner, Michael Brown, Walter Scott, Philando Castile, George Floyd, and so many others should cause some level of emotionality—which can lead to feelings of fear, anxiety, and pain. But as you teach your children, you too must find ways to channel those feelings into positive action. You do have power and control over some things in your life. You do not have to sit idle and wait for a racist act to happen to your children. As discussed previously, there are buffers that can protect children from the mental health consequences of personalized and systemic racism. Simply teaching your children about their rich history and culture and surrounding them with positive influences can make a difference. In addition, you have the power to help dismantle structural racism. This type of systemic change requires (1) an awareness of the laws, policies, and practices that hurt and/or disproportionately impact communities of color and children of color; (2) a willingness to mobilize and be a part of the solution to change the status quo; and (3) a commitment to take methodical action steps.

Now more than ever it is easier to be a change agent. Through the Internet and social media, people can track the issues that are important to them. People are able to follow interest groups and policy makers to stay in the know. Social media has also made it easier to bring attention to certain matters and form groups to keep the momentum going. There are also many online resources including toolkits on how to organize town hall meetings, write an opinion editorial, meet with elected officials, and write letters to public officials. With the various platforms available, people can highlight and discuss policies that are directly impacting children and families as well as organize and bring people together to discuss possible solutions to those issues. You do not have to start from scratch, nor do you have to do it alone. In many communities across America, there are grassroots organizations and nonprofits that have already started the work but are looking for people power and donations to help push the needle forward.

Your voice maters. People of color make up almost 40 percent of America's population. Working together, with allies of different races, can change systems. According to an article posted on the Brookings Institute website:

- Black people have the highest voter turnout compared to other racial groups.

- In 2008, Black voter turnout was within one percentage point of Whites and was actually higher than Whites in 2012.[49]

The article "Five Myths About Black Voters" remarks that for the past 30 years, the Democratic presidential candidate who received the most primary support from Black voters won the party's nomination. All but one—John F. Kerry in 2004—won the popular vote in the general election.[50] According to Pew Research Center, in 2020 Latinos are expected, for the first time, to be the largest racial or ethnic minority in a U.S. presidential election, with a record

32 million projected voters. Blacks will account for 30 million eligible voters.[51]

These numbers are clear evidence that collectively you can make a difference. However, making informed decisions at the polls, and holding the elected accountable, matters.

At the local level, the same degree of participation and energy is required. It is your local officials, school board members, state governors, and state representatives who are making policy decisions that directly affect you and your children. Furthermore, if you are not happy with the slate of candidates running for office or believe that you have the drive and ambition that is needed to advocate on behalf of children and families, you should consider running for office. There are also many resources that are available to get you started: the NPR Life Kit "How to Run for Office," She Should Run, Veterans Campaign, Run for Something, and the Campaign Workshop, to name a few.

Learn How to Protect and Restore Your Peace

Racial stressors can lead to serious health consequences. Studies show that expectant mothers who experienced racism during pregnancy were more likely to have poorer birth outcomes. According to U.S. Department of Health and Human Services Office of Minority Health,

- Adult Blacks/African Americans are more likely to report serious psychological distress than adult Whites.

- Adult Blacks/African Americans living below poverty are three times more likely to report serious psychological distress than those living above poverty.

- Adult Blacks/African Americans are more likely to have feelings of sadness, hopelessness, and worthlessness than are adult Whites.[52]

Hence, finding ways to restore good mental health and rejuvenate your mind and soul is essential. You cannot afford to get burned out, nor can you afford to allow negative energy to consume you. You must shelter your mind and spirit, which may require you to turn off the news and social media and fill that time with positive alternatives.

"Whatever things are true, whatever things are noble, whatever things are just, whatever things are pure, whatever things are lovely, whatever things are of good report, if there is any virtue and if there is anything praiseworthy — meditate on these things." — Philippians 4:8

Practice speaking about yourself in a positive way, and do not be ashamed to let your children hear you. Hang up Post-it notes or pieces of art with positive personal declarations about yourself and your family members throughout your home. Encourage yourself, and refrain from focusing on what you perceive to be your blemishes and shortcomings—instead focus more on what you have to offer and positive action steps that can make your life and your family's lives better. As you make a conscious decision to change your thought process and habits, you may also have to delete certain social media groups and find new friendship circles. Follow the same rules and guidelines that you have set for your children. This includes being selective about people whom you let into your life, and surrounding yourself with positive influences—people who will be honest with you, who will listen to you, but who will also encourage your growth and enjoy hearing the positive things that are happening in your life. Because you have put yourself in an environment filled with people who you love and who love you— you can be open and vulnerable with these people. You are there to help and support them and vice versa. Do not be afraid or embarrassed to ask the people in your circle for help when needed or to speak your truth.

If you are still feeling overwhelmed, hopeless, or just emotionally drained from life and are unable to find healthy ways to cope with your emotions, consult with a therapist or medical professional. It is vital that you find ways to restore your equilibrium— to regain your peace so that you can be whole, and your children can also be whole. You have the power to take control over your life and your mental health.

Taking on Racism While Simplifying Your Life and Reducing Stress

Life can be overwhelming, and most parental figures do not have time to add anything else on their to-do list. This book was written and designed with that in mind. Because many parental figures struggle with balancing what is already on their plates, the thought of finding time to learn about Black history, teach your children that history, become actively involved in your community, and somehow find time for yourself to meditate and restore may seem impossible. If that is the case, and you have the means, consider hiring other people to help lighten the load by stepping in to clean your home, run errands, help you with your finances, or suggest a more realistic schedule that you can feel good about. For others, remember you do not have to do everything at once. Find a few hours and write out what is most important and build around those things. Learn to let go of those things and people that do not fit into that plan. This will be different for each family, but what must be included on the list is taking the time to love yourself—taking the time to ensure that your children also love who they are—and that their love is deeply rooted in an understanding of their history. If you can start with that and master it, the psychological harms of racism will be greatly reduced.

ENDNOTES

1   Y. Dunham, A. S. Baron, and M. R. Banaji, "The Development of Implicit Intergroup Cognition," *Trends in Cognitive Science* 12, no. 7 (July 2008): 248–53, doi: 10.1016/j.tics.2008.04.006.

2   J. Williams, D. Best, and D. Boswell, "The Measurement of Children's Racial Attitudes in the Early School Years," *Child Development*, 46, no. 2 (1975): 494–500, doi:10.2307/1128147.

3   Kiri Davis, *A Girl Like Me*, (2005), https://www.reelworks.org/rw/.

4   CNN, "Readers: Children Learn Attitudes about Race at Home" (2010), https://www.cnn.com/2010/US/05/19/doll.study.reactions/index.html.

5   R. Tumaini et al., "Perceived Racial/Ethnic Discrimination Among Fifth-Grade Students and Its Association With Mental Health," *American Journal of Public Health* 99 (2009): 878–884, https://doi.org/10.2105/AJPH.2008.144329.

6   Equal Justice Initiative, "Racial Harassment in Schools Surged in 2017" (March 2018), https://eji.org/news/racial-harassment-schools-surged-2017/. Citing data from the U.S. Department of Education Civil Rights Division.

7   Deidre McPhillips, "Hidden Harms of Racial Bullying," *U.S. News* (May 2019), analyzing 2017-18 data from the California Healthy Kids Survey.

8   Caryn C. Park, "Young Children Making Sense of Racial and Ethnic Differences: A Sociocultural Approach," *American Educational Research Journal* 48, no. 2 (April 2011): 387–420. https://doi.org/10.3102/0002831210382889.

9   Maupin Gilliam et al., "Do Early Educators' Implicit Biases Regarding Sex and Race Relate to Behavior Expectations and Recommendations of Preschool Expulsions and Suspensions? Yale University Child Study Center (September 2016), https://marylandfamiliesengage.org/wp-content/uploads/2019/07/Preschool-Implicit-Bias-Policy-Brief.pdf.

10 P. A. Goff et al., "The Essence of Innocence: Consequences of Dehumanizing Black Children," *Journal of Personality and Social Psychology 106*, no. 4 (2014): 526–545, https://doi.org/10.1037/a0035663.

11   Rebecca Epstein, Jamilia J. Blake, and Thalia González, *Girlhood Interrupted: The Erasure of Black Girls' Childhood* (Washington, DC, Georgetown University Law Center, 2017), http://arks.princeton.edu/ark:/88435/dsp01tx31qm28z.

12   Libby Nelson and Dara Lind, "The School-to-Prison Pipeline, Explained," Justice Policy Institute (February 2015), http://www.justicepolicy.org/news/8775.

13   Tom Rudd, "Racial Disproportionality in School: Implicit Bias is Heavily Implicated," Kirwan Institute Issue Brief (February 2014), https://kirwaninstitute.osu.edu/sites/default/files/2014-02//racial-disproportionality-schools-02.pdf.

14   Nelson and Lind, "The School-to-Prison Pipeline."

15   Nelson and Lind, "The School-to-Prison Pipeline."

16   National Center for Education Statistics, "Table 204.90, Percentage of Public School Students Enrolled in Gifted and Talented Programs by Sex, Race/Ethnicity, and State: Selected Years 2004 through 2013-14," https://nces.ed.gov/programs/digest/d17/tables/dt17_204.90.asp.

17   Jason Grissom and Christopher Redding, "Discretion and Disproportionality: Explaining the Underrepresentation of High-Achieving Students of Color in Gifted Programs," *AERA Open* (2016), https://journals.sagepub.com/doi/10.1177/2332858415622175.

18   Grissom and Redding, "Discretion and Disproportionality."

19   Kristen Harper, "5 Things to Know about Racial and Ethnic Disparities in Special Education," Child Trends (January 2017), https://www.childtrends.org/publications/5-things-to-know-about-racial-and-ethnic-disparities-in-special-education.

20   Arionne Nettles and Monica Eng, "Having 'The Talk': Expert Guidance on Preparing Kids for Police Interactions," NPR WBEZ, (August 2019).

21   Black Youth Project, "Know Your Rights" (March 2010), http://blackyouthproject.com/know-your-rights/.

22   John Gramlich, "The Gap between the Number of Blacks and Whites in Prison is Shrinking," Pew Research Center (April 2019), https://www.pewresearch.org/fact-tank/2019/04/30/shrinking-gap-between-number-of-blacks-and-whites-in-prison/.

23   Ashley Nellis, "The Color of Justice: Racial and Ethnic Disparity in State Prisons," The Sentencing Project (June 2016), https://www.sentencingproject.org/publications/color-of-justice-racial-and-ethnic-disparity-in-state-prisons/.

24   Police Shooting Database 2015-2020, *Washington Post*.

25   Leila Morsy et al., "How Does Our Discriminatory Criminal Justice System
     Affect Children?" Economic Policy Institute (Dec. 21, 2016), https://www.epi.
     org/publication/how-does-our-discriminatory-criminal-justice-system-affect-
     children-black-children-are-six-times-as-likely-as-white-children-to-have-a-
     parent-whos-been-incarcerated/.

26   "Black Disparities in Youth Incarceration, 2015," The Sentencing Project,
     (September 2017), https://www.sentencingproject.org/publications/black-
     disparities-youth-incarceration/.

27   "Black Disparities in Youth Incarceration, 2015."

28   Wendy Sawyer, "Youth Confinement: The Whole Pie 2019," Prison Policy
     Initiative (December 2019), https://www.prisonpolicy.org/reports/youth2019.
     html.

29   Nina Martin and Renne Montagne, "Black Mothers Keep Dying After Giving
     Birth. Sharon Irving's Story Explains Why," NPR (December 2017), https://www.
     npr.org/2017/12/07/568948782/black-mothers-keep-dying-after-giving-birth-
     shalon-irvings-story-explains-why.

30   Caitlin Young, "These Five Facts Reveal the Current Crisis in Black
     Homeownership," Urban Institute (July 2019), https://www.urban.org/urban-
     wire/these-five-facts-reveal-current-crisis-black-homeownership.

31   Emma Garcia, "Schools Are Still Segregated, and Black Children Are Paying
     a Price," Economic Policy Institute, (February 2020), https://www.epi.org/
     publication/schools-are-still-segregated-and-black-children-are-paying-a-price/.

32   National Child Traumatic Stress Network, Justice Consortium, Schools
     Committee, and Culture Consortium, *Addressing Race and Trauma in the
     Classroom: A Resource for Educators* (Los Angeles, CA, and Durham, NC:
     National Center for Child Traumatic Stress, 2017), citing Comas-Diaz, 2016.

33   American Academy of Pediatrics, "Exposure to Racism Harms
     Children's Health," ScienceDaily (2017), www.sciencedaily.com/
     releases/2017/05/170504083210.htm.

34   Congressional Black Caucus Emergency Task Force on Black Youth Suicide
     and Mental Health, *Ring the Alarm: The Crisis of Black Youth Suicide (December
     2019),* https://watsoncoleman.house.gov/uploadedfiles/full_taskforce_report.
     pdf.

35   "Suicide Crises Among Black Youth," The Reach Institute, (February 13, 2020),
     https://www.thereachinstitute.org/newsletters/173-suicide-crisis-among-black-
     youth.

36   Victor Armstrong "Stigma Regarding Mental Illness among People of Color," National Council for Behavioral Health (July 2019), https://www.thenationalcouncil.org/BH365/2019/07/08/stigma-regarding-mental-illness-among-people-of-color/.

37   "Black and African American Communities and Mental Health," Mental Health America, (2021), https://www.mhanational.org/issues/black-and-african-american-communities-and-mental-health.

38   "Black/African American," National Alliance on Mental Illness, https://www.nami.org/Your-Journey/Identity-and-Cultural-Dimensions/Black-African-American.

39   Kristen Harper and Deborah Temkin, "Compared To Majority White Schools, Majority Black Schools Are More Likely to Have Security Staff," Child Trends Blog (April 2018), https://www.childtrends.org/blog/compared-to-majority-white-schools-majority-black-schools-are-more-likely-to-have-security-staff.

40   "How to Build Buffers Against ACEs and Their Consequences," National Institute for Children's Health Quality, https://www.nichq.org/insight/how-build-buffers-against-aces-and-their-consequences.

41   "Mental Illness and the Family: Recognizing Warning Signs and How to Cope," Mental Health America, https://www.mhanational.org/recognizing-warning-signs.

42   Congressional Black Caucus Emergency Task Force on Black Youth Suicide and Mental Health, *Ring the Alarm.*

43   Travis Nixon, "A Dangerous Distortion of Our Families, Representations of Families, by Race, in News and Opinion Media," Color of Change, (January 2018), https://colorofchange.org/dangerousdistortion.

44   Nixon, "A Dangerous Distortion of Our Families."

45   Troy G. Deskins, "Stereotypes in Video Games and How They Perpetuate Prejudice," *McNair Scholars Research Journal* 6, no.1, (2013), http://commons.emich.edu/mcnair/vol6/iss1/5.

46   V. Rideout et al.,"Children, Media, and Race: Media Use among White, Black, Hispanic, and Asian American Children," Center on Media and Human Development School of Communication Northwestern University, (June 2011), https://dcmp.org/learn/301-children-media-and-race-media-use-among-white-black-hispanic-and-asian-american-children.

47   Congressional Black Caucus Emergency Task Force on Black Youth Suicide
      and Mental Health, *Ring the Alarm: The Crisis of Black Youth Suicide (December
      2019)*, https://watsoncoleman.house.gov/uploadedfiles/full_taskforce_report.
      pdf.

48   Matt Thompson, "Five Reasons Why People Code-Switch," NPR (April 2013),
      https://www.npr.org/sections/codeswitch/2013/04/13/177126294/five-reasons-
      why-people-code-switch.

49   Rashawn Ray and Mark Whitlock, "Setting the Record Straight on Black Voter
      Turnout," Brookings (September 2019), https://www.brookings.edu/blog/
      how-we-rise/2019/09/12/setting-the-record-straight-on-black-voter-turnout/.

50   Theodore Johnson, "Five Myths about Black Voters," *Washington Post* (December
      2019).

51   Jen Krogstad and Mark Lopez, "Latino Voters' Interest in Presidential Race is
      Mixed, and About Half are 'Extremely Motivated' to Vote", NPR (October 2020).

52   U.S. Department of Health and Human Services Office of Minority Health,
      "Mental and Behavioral Health—African Americans," https://minorityhealth.
      hhs.gov/omh/browse.aspx?lvl=4&lvlid=24.